Tears of Honey and Gold

Jacqueline Karp

www.fiveleaves.co.uk

Tears of Honey and Gold

Jacqueline Karp

Published in 2004 by Five Leaves Publications,
PO Box 81, Nottingham NG5 4ER
info@fiveleaves.co.uk, www.fiveleaves.co.uk

Five Leaves acknowledges financial assistance
from Arts Council England

Design and typesetting by Four Sheets Design and Print
Printed by Print Quarter in Nottingham

ISBN: 0907123 554

For Régis,
who drove while I wrote

Contents

Other Books by Jacqueline Karp

Poetry
Sudden Maraschinos
Redbeck Press (April 2004)

Non-fiction
Two Hundred Years of Civil Code.
Translation from the French of the book
by Jacques Bouineau and Jérôme Roux,
published online on the website of the
French Ministry of Foreign Affairs Publications
www.adpf.asso.fr (October 2004)

Acknowledgements

Some of these poems were previously published under the author's full name: Jacqueline Karp-Gendre.

Acknowledgments with thanks to the editors of magazines where some of the poems first appeared: *Poetry and Audience, The Nude in Mae's Cupboard* (Biscuit Top Twenty Anthology 2004), *Cumberland Review, European Judaism, The Reater, Hampden Sydney Poetry Review, Never Bury Poetry, Poetry Nottingham International, Poems of the World*, and to Rita Eustace for the genesis of "Fax to J".

Also in this pamphlet series

I Could Become That Woman *Sibyl Ruth*
(0907123546)
Last Hour of Sleep *Naomi Jaffa* (0907123740)
Flood Warning *Berta Freistadt* (0907123945)
Choose Your Frog *Harold Rosen* (090712335X)

Fax to: J.

From: a pre-installed user
re: ghosts

And what about Mérida? Was that train delayed once
or a thousand times? How often
did we cross the line? All those people,
a whole transhumance. And the nappies on the track.
The heat and the dark and the unknown.
And when it did come, that one-eyed monster
out of the night, and we reached up to it,
the guards with guns who would not let us in.
Somehow the press of bodies took us on
and we were in some *terrine portugaise*,
proximity and smell of flesh — undesired,
undesirable — overwhelm me even to this day.
Remember?
Tell me about it.

Bisous électroniques, RRRRRRRRR.

Tales from the Guggenheim

Frank Gehry's Guggenheim sleeps
along the Nervión, a tired dinosaur
not quite sure where to stretch.

He tucks arms and legs beneath
him, flops his clanking carapace
into a silvery hotchpotch
of limb and haunch
and gleams a gentle night glow.

Opposite, beneath the sewage smell,
surprised houses blink at him
through grey Cantabrian drizzle.

Inside, space swirls about, stressed
in pale rays of green, enclosing us
in nowhere exactly, but sending the eye
up and round and out again

to the cold muddy Nervión
where the dinosaur sleeps.

***

What I liked best were Clemente's illustrations[1]
of Ginsberg's poems,
handwritten by the poet on a scrawny New York afternoon,
(some afternoon!)
the poet's writing scrawly and with forgotten words
squashed slanting in from above like curly smoke from
sinking chimney pots
or old black trains shunting into a siding,
and all around, Clemente's childlike boys
catching their translucent dreams in their puppy dog cheeks
before they run away.

---

[1]*Francesco Clemente Exhibition, Bilbao, February 2000*

But how does the guard
in stern red jacket and tight grey skirt
spend her long day
surrounded by this plethora
of wine red penises
and row upon row of see-through yet
dreamily vague vaginas
as colourful as a Caribbean market?

The large black cat in the next canvas
crouches in a corner
weeping tears of honey and gold.

***

Two large woolly things
called *Dulce de leche*[2]
by Mabi Revuelta,
a young Bilbao artist, the Basque title *Esne-gozokia*
and the description "stained steel and mohair"
giving nothing away about
how strokeable these creatures are.
They hang
like giant curds from the silver sky
creamy udders
out of bounds
that just slightly swing
and glow
in the breathless museum air
before another scarlet guard
who stands so close
they could be her shaggy breasts.

I would love to milk her.

---

[2]*blancmange*

A Quiet Night

At Salamanca, a mile or so north
from the bypass, the Zamora road,
stands La Capea, a one-star place.
For our first night, it'll have to do.

It's deserted, yet from every fir,
loudspeakers greet us, that good Iberian
mix of Radio Uno chit-chat, *jotas*,
Spanish pop, enough to deafen any normal ear.

In her darkened office, the *señora*
mouths me a lipsticked *Buenas*,
takes my ID, fixes a tired smile.
The whining voices do not bother her.

We pick a distant sandy pitch
among the early flowering mint,
the whole air rich with almond scent
and mauving lavender spikes.

The early evening brings its thunder-claps,
downpours, the usual power cuts.
By ten, it's lorries changing gears
right beside us.

Long after one the night is rent
by a high-pitched woman's voice
confronting a man's,
his low, menacing, persistent.

Near dawn, I'm woken by a whooping sound,
and over breakfast see the hoopoe splash
his crest and fleeting plumage:
white black blush.

In the washroom silence
a died blonde shouts
"*Hola, soy Belen!*"
then starts to bleach her roots.

Pine Nuts and Angel's Hair[1]

In the convent of Las Dueñas, the cloister capitals
flash horrible long tongues, great shining eyes
bulge forth over strong out-thrust chests.
These are the muscle men, frolicking
naked in the afternoon sun,
mocking young novices who scrub
and clean the cloister at day's end,
their young frames throbbing
with passion never quenched.

Maybe at night, when young nuns are tucked
trembling in their beds,
those wiry little satyrs slide
from their narrow ledges
to tiptoe through the long quiet dormitories
and pulling back rough blankets,
slip between the plain white sheets
and secretly bring joy beneath
those long protective skirts.

That must be why these days the cloister's
closed to nuns. Visitors may ogle
at the folds of carved contorted flesh
and the present fashion is for wedding
photographs of pure white brides
snapped right alongside scenes of
hellfire, damnation, mortal sin.
A timely warning? It keeps the nuns
from wishing and the coffers full.

Sister Dolores, plump and plain
beneath that stern white veil, and safe,
enclosed behind her wall of glass,
has found a substitute for lust.
She hasn't scrubbed that cloister floor in years;
instead she sells the tourists
little balls of sheer delight —
roasted pine nuts, marzipan, angel's hair —
She can't believe it's sinful to taste that.

Salamanca

---

[1]*Angel's hair,* cabello de ángel = *melon used for jam*

Tierras sin Pan[1]

Miranda del Castañar
just hangs there somehow
on the edge of things,
face set west towards
Las Hurdes and to Portugal.

No petrol-station yet,
one small *supermercado*,
a lady selling honey —
"*Eucalipto y tomillo, señora...*"
hazelnut brown in the noon.

There's the great square,
empty still, awaiting visitors;
beyond, the handcraft shop —
slim black pots, willow baskets,
all labelled at a decent price.

Here history paid a visit
then moved on. Poverty too.
Instead, Tourist Board inscriptions
"Best Floral Village" prizes,
acres of cherry trees in bloom.

Have they forgotten?
Those days of *tierras sin pan*
when milk and chestnuts
— now the local speciality —
was once survival food?

Today the baker bakes a fine wheat flour;
he sells us two round fragrant loaves
with smooth gold crust and creamy white inside,
but crossed with long deep scars
just like the land.

---

[1]*Land without Bread: Title of Luis Buñuel's 1930s documentary on poverty in Las Hurdes*

Cáceres

Cáceres, Sunday afternoon,
and it's a steep climb
to the first empty square,
the narrow lanes brooding
in yellow sandstone.

A tattered beggar stands
outside the church
as bells call out for mass.
A nun in navy blue walks
briskly past him on the other side.

Crumbling coats of arms cling
to an ancient wall.

I'd like to know,
behind these great shut doors
do hunger-thin hidalgos still live on,
still chew gold toothpicks
and wait for some post-modern Lazarillo
to steal a scrap of food for them?

Return

Guadalupe was a pale postcard.
Crumpled.

The asphalt montage
fragile.

Cafés, cash dispensers
and the grocer:

“They’ve purified the olives
in our oil.”

I looked in at the hotel. No-one
by the pool.

No wonder you didn’t
recognise it.

Clam Fishing

One hand raised to plunge the pole, the other pulling
down.
So rhythmical. A timeless gesture,
this ploughing of sand,
treasured knowledge a father passes
to his son, so each may line the shore,
drag sand and shell into his nets
and eke a living out against the tide.

They must have stood here,
harvesting *coquinas*[1],
that day when further down the coast
those three ships sailed.
When they stopped, beaten by the waves,
did they look out towards La Rábida
and watch three caravels race west into the unknown?

Matalascañas, Huelva

---

[1]*small elongated clam*

Porphyrio Porphyrio

Knee-deep all day in marsh and grass-fringed lake,
his only habitat high beds of cane,
the purple gallinule is limited to southern Spain
where he can hide among the dense dry brakes.

His upper-parts are clad in purple-blue
— his plumage is as royal as king or queen's —
while on his throat and breast the damask sheen
is shot in sunlight with a turquoise hue.

The legs and frontal shield are stunning red
— though undertail and coverts are pure white —
deep as a cardinal's silk robe and quite
as rich, when out he pops from his reed bed.

And here he lurks; he seldom swims, just eats.
It takes him all his time to balance so
one leg set firm in mud, the other claw
articulated for this tricky feat

of fishing in the reeds for lime-green shoots
— he's quite unbeaten over etiquette —
with that gloved hand so red and delicate
he holds each morsel like asparagus.

Not north nor south he flies, but munches here
and thus he must have munched and crunched and died
mated and crunched and munched again and died
since waters flowed down the Guadalquivir.

So, did he witness from his marshy crib
— cradled between the river and the sea —
the flow of Jews and Muslim refugees
sailing downstream, heading for the Maghrib?

Of course he may have heard the loud report
of splintering wood from autos-da-fé upstream,
— Raucous magpies? A heron in the reeds?
Just noisy egrets? — he must have thought.

But did the sickly scent of charring human meat,
flamingos wheeling up in bright pink swarms
to flee the acrid fumes, the peck he gave at scraps of limb
bobbing past, set off his eerie, hooting shriek?

Doñana National Park

Inheritance

They've hung them on the wall in Mérida —
great charcoal-grey and white mosaics, which
seen thus, look more like tribal carpets
and are easier to read.
I'd thought till then the Romans so methodical,
all symmetry and balance, nothing improvised
or out of place:
columns, archways, amphitheatres
enclosing space
with such monotonous precision.

So I was glad to see these old mosaic floors
and find unfinished patterns taper off
at bottom edge, rectangular designs
not quite as parallel as should have been
an extra lozenge here or there
not corresponding.
They must have pieced them square by square
like women weaving carpets, some vague idea
sketched out on parchment, a minor task memorised,
performed by mere apprentices,
only the central coloured artwork
left to the master craftsman.

I watched a workman in the street outside
assemble stones and pebbles
— each a different colour shape or size —
some red, some yellow, oval, round or square,
and set them out with care in wet cement
to make great swirling patterns on the ground.
He felt each pebble, weighed each in his palm
then placed them carefully in snaking lines
to make a modern walkway through the town.
No two whorls the same. Each one a work of art.
And from which I wondered, had he then
inherited his lack of symmetry:
from Moorish carpets or from Roman tiles?

Mérida Roman Art Museum

Landscape with Olive Stumps

It's Spring, and we have travelled miles, mile
upon blood-red mile, but still the same stumps,
still the feeble wisps of olive branch
punctuate the hills' vermilion.

The cork trees too, their hearts plucked out,
droop their green arms or dance, now stripped,
their smooth black-stockinged legs
leaping half-crazed across the empty fields.

Here are no tillers. No peasant women
dressed in black. No mules. A few sleek bulls
grazing the landscape, walls enclosing
nothing, gates leading nowhere.

Hunger-harsh Extremadura, that sent *conquistadors*
across the sea to plunder, rape, destroy,
now waits it turn: corks to be stripped, olives
pollarded, black bulls to the ring.

And yet it's Spring and you can almost hear the warm earth
pushing up the cobalt bells of borage, spreading
the mallow, setting bright lavender to sparkle mauve,
speckling pastures with sudden gold, softening the
background.

Córdoba

From clustered leaves of eucalyptus
glaucous fingers strum
        an ancient air
rustling out memories
        some dusty dreamtime tune
from a lost continent.

In the *mezquita*, arabesques of stone
chiselled in rough
        swirling horseshoes
trace a damask rose
        or some forgotten desert star
long hidden in its geometric prose.

On precious parchments, strings of words
uttered by Christian,
                Muslim, Jew
weave simple lines
of understanding, faint
mutual syllables rescued from a plundered past.

Monastery of Yuste[1]

After so many battles and that mad mother to boot
it was only right he should end here:
soft rays of light cast through the shady trees,
quiet blue of scattered borage clumps,
sun flashed off the Gredos snows above
his only company.
                    Did he come in search of peace?
Or mere monotony? Same sounds, same smells,
same looks exchanged — were they a need?
The slow dull honk of distant bells,
the soothing drip of water in the pond,
sharp mountain thyme and secretive wild mint,
the same monks bringing him his daily food.

Could he thus forget? The wars, Pavia
and the captured king, *germanías* and *comuneros*
put down with all that blood and butchery.
Or Augsburg? His failure in the eyes of God.
Cuio regio cuio religio — that fool's concession
long regretted now — his empire shared
by Luther and the Pope. Hadn't he
done better here in Spain?
Autos-de-fé for all those heretics,
the crypto-Muslims, sly Marranos,
mass baptisms, more unity that way.
And eased his conscience thus before the Lord.
And so he journeyed back, riddled by debts
and gout, to the country he loved least.
A reconciliation with his own intolerance?
Flanders forgotten? Erasmus too?

I picked bright mallow leaves and borage bells
beneath the high stone wall and shady trees,
survivors of the monastery destroyed, rebuilt,
the endless visitors. More searchers for peace?

---

[1]*It was here that Charles V retired after abdicating to his son, Philip II, and where he died a few months later in 1556.*

Concierto de Aranjuez

Tap… tap… slowly the white stick taps, counts one
by one the battered metal seats, catches
in wooden grooves, then lurches into space
and leads its owner down into the sharp sun.
Last stop. Far end of the campus. I'm late.
We are the last two in the tram
in chilly December Madrid. I take his arm.
With my beginner's Spanish, we chat.

I can still see him. Dark little man: rough coat,
black glasses. Up the dusty marble stairs
we went, me pushing him through the morning rush.
"Joaquín Rodrigo, Music Professor" on the door meant

nothing. Now when I listen to his *Concierto de Aranjuez*
I still don't know how in 1938
the bombs, the distant rifle shots,
didn't reach his ears, even in far off France,

or how he heard only the milky green water
and the shafts of light and plucked those soft ripples…
but then maybe in wartime only a blind man could dapple
the Tagus with his urgent guitar.

Bringing in the Catch

Death comes striped here
in blue shot turquoise silk,
so many thousands, you turn away
from the mountain of death, the sea raped.

They swing the crates high over the quay,
shining with firm-bellied
plunder — mackerel
upon shark-tailed mackerel.

And here come the red-headed wives
mini skirts and fag in mouth
rushing loud laughter across the cobbles
to drag the crates to auction.

The men rest against bollards smoking;
they talk of their night at sea.
The apprentice sits
shoulders hunched, eyes shut.

San Vicente de la Barquera

Blooming

At the greengrocer's at Cabezón de la Sal,
brand-new white-tiled shop
on the wet way out of town,
the parsley
is so tired waiting for custom
it has sl-
id off
the shelf, each stalk
clinging
to the next
like a
string
of
doomed
mountaineers.

The cabbages have boxed all night and lost
— their yellow leaves now mottled and bruised —
and the frightened peas have shrivelled
to the far end of their crate.

Only the greengrocer girl is blooming:
melon-breasts, asparagus-fingers, apricot-cheeks.
Over the white tiled counter she watches
the bent women labour back
from the cheaper market stalls,
their nylon bags cutting
through old chapped flesh.

Friday Was Full of Visigoths

Friday was full of Visigoths, their rows
of ochre colonnades, rope-twisted, perched
sideways to Oviedo's dull damp sprawl:
Santa María del Naranco — church

or summer palace? Experts can't decide.
Seventy thousand stones — no two alike
built as they build their pasture walls today,
thin ones next to thick, for balance and might.

The guide jabs at her watch, "*Es la uuuuuu*
na, la una." Jangles her heavy keys.
We shrug shoulders and stand firm. Capitu-

lating, she reinstates her public smile,
sells us two last tickets. A bargain has
been struck. She starts again. "*Santa María del…*

Success

Yesterday we upped and went,
"Once it's all wet, it's all wet," you said. Spent

two hours in silence.
Drove nearly to Palencia.

Rain just as bad, the Meseta oozing
dog-shit yellow mud. You, mad. While munching

our rain-splashed picnic,
you remark,

"Well, your idea of heading south
was frankly a success."

That sent us back. We reached
Fromisto, discovered its Romanesque church

sitting like a perfect round
of fresh baked farmhouse bread,

apse upon apse latched
like limpet buns each to the next.

An Ordinary Day

It has been an ordinary day
— ®*Fruit 'n Fibre* for you, ®*Shredded Wheat*
for me — and that mound of salad you
tucked into for supper. But I don't

want to forget the old man trotting
down the road on his four-legged clogs
like a Moroccan teapot going
for a walk, black brollie under arm

or the thin lady at the baker's
buying her first loaf of wholemeal bread:
"No, *señora*, it won't make you fat."

And the tremble in her voice, "*Bueno,
bueno*, if you say it won't."

Drought

Gandarilla church boasts a plaque to *indianos*,
emigrants gone to Cuba for "God and the race".

We leave its shade, to walk through the hamlet,
the warm valley above alive with clinking bells.

A grey-haired lady in her late fifties sits
in her yard. "*Qué tiempo más seco!*" She can't

recall a Spring like this. Her face is sad.
"On holiday?" We nod. "We never go away."

She points up at the jangling pastures. "Only God knows,
we've never had a drought like this." Across the lane,

an old man crouches, weeding to Shostakovich
full blast on his stereo. The village,

apart from them, is deserted. At Casa Pedro,
another man, red face and turquoise shirt,

just leans against his fence, looking from sky
to parched field, then at the barren sky again.

Campside Jottings 1

Ten thirty. The gas lamp, incandescent,
whistles a rasping tune, allows us
to read surrounded by the night. Families
of Spaniards have arrived for the weekend

from Santander. The wind, intermittent,
sends us laughter, mopeds, dogs, urgent loud
masculine conversation. Gathered clouds
gently sway the orange shrouds of our tent.

The first drops come singly and insistent.
El Diario forecast *chubascos*.[1]
Now loud squalls swell the billowing canvas.

And I wonder if the lady is content.
Is Shostakovich still playing to the hills?
And the farmer still staring at his field?

---

[1]*showers*

Campsite Jottings 2

Was it the wind blowing through our hair, indigo breakers rising like foaming cobras and lashing out at us above the cliffs, or because we were together? You are my active muse, you take ten steps for every thought I have, striding past long empty beaches and the homeless man drunk and sleeping off his drunken night against a tree and me trailing behind.

Did you see him? Or notice the poets set in bronze? Gerardo Diego, Fernández Moreno, Río del Sainz, all guarding the wide bay. I breathe in the north here, Cantabria, en route for Asturias, glass-fronted against the Atlantic gales.

While you sit reading, a mouse has just hopped past your foot, his silky fur almost black

and somewhere in the night a toad is croaking.

Santander

The Smell of Wheat

What do I miss? I don't know really,
I don't miss home, not
what you could call miss it,
left too young to have taken root
really but there are things I miss...
like the swish of eucalyptus and the food,
the shellfish, in La Coruña.
we were by the sea, and so I really miss
the fish and especially the shellfish, not the same
here in London, so expensive

and also, when I was a little girl
I remember the smell of the wheat
in the summer, my mother takes us
down to the mill with the wheat
to be milled on a stone mill
and I remember the smell
of the fresh ground wheat
and when the dough swells
we go to the baker's oven, such a huge furnace
where our bread is baked crusty and hard,
but we didn't come
just from a village we were from the town,
though in the summer we spent the holidays
in the country, I remember also the taste
of that bread long and thin like French bread
or (*thinking*) Italian and (*punching fist into palm*)
the sea, the force of the Atlantic

that I miss and now my husband gone
— cirrhosis of the liver, a liberation —
now my life can begin, him I really don't miss.

New Warmth

we are leaving behind
Les Corbières, expectant vines
green and fluffy yellow green

leaving behind
the glower of rain
and now see patches of blue
stretching the clouds open
like pulled muffins

warmth of sun through glass
and my shoulder aching
across the car for you

abandoned sheep pens, their stone walls
like broken rings
thrown on a threadbare rug
and just in sight, the sea,

and long lagoons.

The Pyrenees, running out of breath,
hiccup out a few stony excrescences
and become Spain.

Rivesaltes

Sweet wine. Today only oranges
rumble north from Orihuela
past where the old internment camp
did its job.

Old?

Oh! The Spanish reds are gone
and the Jews and the French communists and after that
came of course *collabos*[1]
and later still the *harkis*[2] and some *Sénégalais*.

Did?

And there's still a corner of the camp in use
... isn't a camp always useful for something?
A few illegal *sans papiers*[3] on their way here
or on their way home or just on their way...

(the word *indésirables* is not used any more)

and anyway it's a far corner, well out of sight
and the mountains not jagged enough
to goad our easy amnesia, smooth
shouldered ridges smiling nice two dimensional smiles

flattened
like the cardboard bottle billboards
for : *RIVESALTES —*
VIN DOUX NATUREL

---

[1]*Second World War collaborators.*
[2]*Algerian regiments who fought with the French and had to flee Algeria on independence.*
[3]*Undocumented immigrants.*

Waiting

Along the flowering hillside
crouch the trees,
crippled by tramontana winds,
bent landward.

Their grey arms embrace a dusty wall
or brush against a wrought-iron balcony.
Gnarled olives, wedged into narrow fields,
or leaning over dried-up wadis

— straggle of broken cactus, rotting agaves —
stand as they always have
patient by the old road
where desert meets north.

A church thrusts its warning tower
up to God and young almonds
clutch their slim velvet,
awaiting a rebirth.

But Easter has grown
tired this year. On the old
Gerona highway
wan-faced girls in laddered tights

tout for clients searching
for a quick release
in the littered lay-by
among the crouching trees.

Barcelona

The night porter at the Pelayo Hotel
speaks Spanish with a hobbled voice
that's travelled haltingly from Hungary
to Palestine and on to Chili and
"*Ach, durch die ganze Welt!*" till now he sits
boxed in behind his desk
in windowless seventh floor Barcelona
opening
the door from behind his desk

no worries

no responsibilities
no family

just
opening
and
opening and
opening.

Below him, Barcelona
never sleeps, just dozes to the gargle of diesel,
to the hiss and the shake and the thump
of pneumatic drills gauging huge cavities
from the cities' jaws,

then jolts awake to Vespas that whirr like giant moths
competing with the crack of dawn,
to watermen who swoosh the gutters clean, and wild
music
ghetto-blasting from an open car.

My dreams are thick chocolate
the colour of Gaudí's stone.

By dawn,

a miracle...

the hearthless of the night before, *los sin hogar*,
and the cardboard box constructions
that harboured them through the flimsy night

have evaporated
in the early mist snaking its
way up from the Rambla

and all the shoe shop entrances
sparkle clean

so customers
will never know whose
beds they are
treading
on…

and soon up the hill in the Parc Güell
the kindergarten parties will be out,
chatting excited Catalan,

exercise books bulging
with outlined dragons

to be coloured
with gaudy Gaudí.

But how can you confine a four-year-old
in a dragon mould?

Joan Corominas (1905–1997)

So they found the exile a square. The lines are pure. All brand new and squeaky clean. Not a red-lipped prostitute in sight. Plenty of space

now, with the demolition and Vasquez Montalbán's world gone.

Homage to Catalonia's great linguist, the dictionary man who traced the languages of Spain,
dug up Latin and Arabic roots, drew family trees of words.

On the far side of the draughty arch of something post-post-Modern and shut.

No shade. No lanes. Children curving past on rollers.

And on a low wall that leads to the Contemporary Art Museum, an old Pakistani, white
djellaba, white skull cap, white beard, white eyes, cross-legged, throwing crumbs to the pigeons. Dreaming of Lahore?

Barcelona, December 2002

Conjuro de la Nada

Y una voz clamó en el desierto
— voz de esperanza que iba a llenar de calor los corazones,
voz de esperanza que iba a encender los corazones muertos de sed —
una voz en el desierto.

La mar relucía como una moneda de plata,
revolcábanse las palmeras en la brisa
con sus hojas de verde y azul.
Bajaban sus cabezas para levantarlas
orgullosas, triunfales,
estremeciéndose en esperanza.

El sol ... ¡ay cómo brillaba!
¡Con qué fuerza me calentaba el corazón!

***

De polvo están cubiertas las palmeras.
¿No quieres decirme por qué?
Gris se ha vuelto la mar que brillaba.
¿Y no puedes decirme por qué?

Se calló la voz.
Se calló la voz que clamaba en el desierto.

¡Silencio! Pero no teja la monja.
Llora por su corazón
muerto entre las palmeras polvorientas.
Llora por el engaño del mar gris.
Llora por las lágrimas amargas de la toronja.

In the Bar

In the bar, Aznar, all in blue, mumbles away at us
from his giant screen in the corner. Nobody listens.

The tourist office sells a brochure on
Intolerance in the Reign of Ferdinand and Isabella.

Outside, the hills breathe fenugreek and history.
Far below, the river rumbles. Mopeds imitate

angry insects. On the ramparts, an Italian calls "*Salute*!"
to his sneezing wife. For a second, I hear "*Salaam.*"

A vulture circles over terracotta walls and pale
round Arab tiles. Rounded tail. Thin wing feathers.

Poised, totally indifferent to
the overhead roar of fighter planes.

He's seen it all before: Romans, Visigoths,
Arab, Berber, Aragonese. Republican. Nationalist.

And now Aznar, mouthing his proud policy in Iraq.

Albarracín

Albarracín is an old Berber perch
where the earth must once have cracked
and choked and sighed and tilted up a town.

Behind, in the rock caves, you can almost
see a giant half open an eye and wink at you.
He's guarding the green and white

and blue *mudéjar* towers, the ramparts
placed there like a careful child's building bricks
on the early morning hills. And I half

expect a door to open and a veiled girl set off
down the steep hill, a jar on her head,
or see the men, herding their flocks up to graze

on the rocky pastures above the town, wrap rough
djellabas round them and call out "*Balak*! *Balak*[1]"
as they egg their sheep through the narrow streets.

But I'll make do with *café con leche* in a glass
and the morning's paper full of football
and think of the market man who gave us a cabbage.

Repollo, I'd forgotten the word. "*Repollo*," I whisper back,
hugging it to me, rolling myself in the sound.

---

[1]*Look out!*

Reminders

On the road from Daroca to Calatayud
the hills are the colour of camels.
Dirty. Low. Studded with almond trees.

All that remains of the great Morisco expulsion:
the churches' thin *mudéjar*-style bricks
and a feeling of desolation.

Calatayud itself spurts grey out of the rock
in a series of timorous outgrowths
on the crust of the Meseta.

Then comes the Sierra de la Virgen
where towns called Moros or Almonacid
are all that is left to remind us.

But there's always a ruined castle
and always a church. Where Berbers for
generations harvested the grain,

never a trace of a mosque... Yet early courgettes
and peppers from Almería, and giant
hollow strawberries from Huelva

are still picked by men the same
olive brown as those you'd have found
on the road from Daroca to Calatayud.

Fax to: R.

From: J
re: those ghosts

It wasn't Mérida you know. We'd left Salamanca
on the night train, bound for Aranda de Duero.
The compartments were packed. No lights. Voices
came at us disembodied through the dark.
At Aranda we alighted, to catch the Paris train.
The rest is right. The trains from Lisbon
blocked the Spaniards out. (Secular hatreds
no EC contiguity has yet changed.)
It was the third train we got on, past 3a.m.,
coming from Madrid, so safe. Sat on our cases
as far as Irún, shivered through the night
and breakfasted on cold brain *bocadillo*[1].
Don't you remember?

Bisous électroniques, JJJJJJJJ.

---

[1]*sandwich*